ALONG THE WESTERN ROAD

Perhaps we
will see you back
again some day, after
the steam has run out

Best Wishes
& Good Luck

Jo-Anne & Geoff
March.

Yolande - Kate
Jason & Sam.

ACKNOWLEDGEMENTS

For permission to reprint the material in this anthology the publishers acknowledge the following:

The estate of the late E. J. Brady for "The Western Road" by E. J. Brady.

Hugh Esson for "The Shearer's Wife" by Louis Esson.

F. A. Mecham for "Said Hanrahan" by John O'Brien, from Around the Boree Log and Other Verses, Angus & Robertson Publishers.

The copyright owner for extracts from "The Old Station", "It's Grand", "The Merino Sheep" and "Bush Life" and for the poem "Saltbush Bill J.P." by A. B. Paterson. "It's Grand" and "Saltbush Bill J.P." from The Collected Verse of A. B. Paterson, Angus & Robertson Publishers.

Angus & Robertson Publishers
London • Sydney • Melbourne • Singapore • Manila

First published by Angus & Robertson Publishers, Australia, 1981

© This selection Angus & Robertson Publishers

National Library of Australia
Cataloguing-in-publication data.

Along the western road.

ISBN 0 207 14302 1.

1. Australian literature. I. Lindsay, Percy.

A820'.8

Typeset in 11 pt Bembo by Graphicraft Typesetters
Printed in Hong Kong.

ALONG
THE WESTERN ROAD

Bush Stories and Ballads

Illustrated by
PERCY LINDSAY.

Angus and Robertson Publishers

PERCY LINDSAY

Percival Charles Lindsay was born in 1870 at Creswick, Victoria, the first of the talented family of six sons and four daughters. But, as his brother Daryl writes, "unlike Norman and Lionel he was without personal ambition and the devouring urge to create". He painted for himself because he loved it, and had to be prodded by his family and friends to use his skills to earn a crust.

After "fiddling about with drawing and painting in an amateurish way" he studied art with Walter Withers in 1889. Withers developed and encouraged Percy's natural talent for the landscapes which remained his greatest pleasure throughout life.

At Lionel's urging he left Creswick in 1897 for the bohemian delights of Melbourne, and a precarious but happy existence as a black and white artist (for anyone who would employ him) followed. At the same time he was exhibiting his landscapes with the Victorian Art Society and was a member of the Hanging Committee of that Society.

In 1917 he moved with his wife and son to Sydney and, like Norman, began contributing a steady stream of sketches to The Bulletin. In Sydney he exhibited with the Society of Artists, then a strong body with such names as Julian Ashton, Arthur Streeton, George Lambert, Elioth Gruner and the other Lindsays on the membership.

Although he made a niche for himself with paintings of the Australian landscape that are acclaimed as unique in their lyrical sensitivity, he is also remembered by his family and friends for his light-hearted approach to life. Some, like brother Norman (in a letter to sister Mary) felt this attitude was too light-hearted. "Observe Perce as the effect of a happy childhood. He never in all his life faced up to struggle for self expression or self assertion in conflict with the struggle for existence. He just dodged that by making a joke of it . . . His simple device of taking all men good fellows got rid of taking them seriously."

But there were many "good fellows" who admired his talent for finding life so enjoyable. It was with affection that his Bulletin colleagues wrote of him on his death in 1952:

> "He lived the perfect life for an artist, inhabiting an old stone tenement in North Sydney with battered books, battered furniture, battered teapots, oil-paints, brushes, palettes, easels and lovely little paintings in battered frames all over the place, the latest canvases stuck on the walls for further meditation. He cared absolutely nothing for money, never knew that politics existed, took no part in the warfare of the arts, wanted nothing but what he had: a roof and a bed, something to eat, friends to relax with, and the whole of time free for painting."

It is his warm, human and easy approach to life that is reflected in the lively illustrations presented here.

Contents

From **The Western Road**

MY camp was by the Western Road—so new and yet so old—
The track the bearded diggers trod in roaring days of old;
The road Macquarie and his wife, a hundred years ago,
With warlike guard and retinue, went down in regal show.

The moon had silvered all the Bush; now, like an arc-light high,
She flickered in a scattered scud that dimmed the lower sky;
And, dreaming by my dying fire, whose embers fainter glowed,
I saw their shadows flitting by—the People of the Road.

I heard the clank of iron chains, and, as an evil blast
From some tormented nether world, the convict gangs went past
With sneering lips and leering eyes—grey ghosts of buried crime,
Who built a way for honest feet to tread in later time.

.   .   .   .

But, dreaming by my campfire still, uprose the merry horn;
A heavy stage came lumbering up from Penrith in the morn,
In beaver hats, the gentlemen their driver sat beside,
And ladies in hooped petticoats and quaint chignons inside.

T-ran-ta-ra! Blue Mountains hills re-echoed as they sung
A lilt of love and long ago—when all the world was young.
T-ran-ta-ra! Their shades went by, the bravest and the best,
The first Australian pioneers—whose graves are in the west.

.   .   .   .

White-tilted in the moonlight went rough wagons one by one,
Piled high with household goods and stores of settlers dead and gone—
Blithe British yeomen and their wives, and sons of younger sons,
Who took tradition to the west, and axes, ploughs and guns.

These new-chum settlers tramped beside their dusty, creaking
  teams,
Their minds were filled with marvels new and golden hopes and
  dreams;
Their sons' tall sons still yeomen be, but mostly in the west
They ride their silken thoroughbreds, and ruffle with the best.

A motley crowd of eager folk, with tools and tents in fold
Came on Adventure's early quest to Gulgong, grief and gold;
They passed me in a jostling host, with anger or with mirth,
The fortune-seekers gathered from the ends of all the earth.

Yea, sailormen and tailormen, and prostitutes and peers,
Some honest and of good intent, some rogues and buccaneers.
Their campfires lit the darkened range, where, by the creeks, they
  lay
And dreamed of nuggets in their sleep—impatient for the day.

Came up the road a swaying coach; his ribbons holding free,
The perfect driver tilted back his cherished cabbage-tree.
His girl will meet him at the rails tonight in Hartley Vale—
So, clear the track, and let her pass, the mid-Victorian mail!

Long shadows fell across the road; the mopoke in the still
And solemn midnight voiced aloud his warnings on the hill.
Yet, tramping slow and riding fast along that winding track,
The People of the Road went west, and coached and footed back.

My campfire died in ashes grey, as through my dream there went
That strange procession of the Past, on pay or plunder bent;
The teamsters, drovers, swagmen, lags; the lovers and the thieves—
Until the east was red with dawn, the dew upon their leaves.

They vanished with the haunted night; their hope and high desire
As ashen as the grey, cold heap that erstwhile made my fire.
Across the tree-tops in the morn the golden sunlight showed;
And clearly rose another day—along the Western Road.

                                        E. J. BRADY

THE CONVICT GANGS
WENT PAST

The Convicts' Rum Song

CUT yer name across me backbone,
Stretch me skin across a drum,
Iron me up on Pinchgut Island
From today till Kingdom Come!

I will eat yer Norfolk dumpling
Like a juicy Spanish plum,
Even dance the Newgate Hornpipe
If ye'll only gimme RUM!

ANON

From True Patriots All

FROM distant climes, o'er widespread seas we come,
Though not with much *éclat*, or beat of drum;
True patriots all, for be it understood,
We left our country for our country's good:
No private views disgraced our generous zeal,
What urged our travels was our country's weal:
And none will doubt but that our emigration
Has proved most useful to the British nation.

GEORGE CARTER

Botany Bay, A New Song

LET us drink a good health to our schemers above,
Who at length have contrived from this land to remove
Thieves, robbers and villains, they'll send 'em away,
To become a new people at Botany Bay.

Some men say they have talents and trades to get
  bread,
Yet they spunge on mankind to be cloathed and fed,
They'll spend all they get, and turn night into day,
Now I'd have all such sots sent to Botany Bay.

There's gay powder'd coxcombs and proud dressy
  fops,
Who with very small fortunes set up in great shops,
They'll run into debt with design ne'er to pay,
They should all be transported to Botany Bay.

The tradesman who plays at cards, billiards and dice,
Must pay for their goods an extravagant price,
No faith I'm mistaken such rogues never pay,
Therefore they should all go to Botany Bay.

Many men they are married to good-natur'd wives,
They'll run after wenches and lead debauch'd lives;
Our wise legislature should send such away,
To support their system in Botany Bay.

There's night-walking strumpets who swarms in each
  street
Proclaiming their calling to each man they meet;
They become such a pest that without delay,
These corrupters of youth should be sent to Botany
  Bay.

There's monopolisers who add to their store,
By cruel oppression and squeezing the poor,
There's butchers and farmers get rich quick in that
     way,
But I'd have all such rogues sent to Botany Bay.

We've great men above and gentry below,
They'll talk much of honour, and make a great show,
But yet never think their poor tradesmen to pay,
Such defaulters I'd have sent to Botany Bay.

You lecherous whoremasters who practise vile arts
To ruin young virgins and break parents hearts,
Or from the fond husband the wife leads astray,
Let such debauch'd stallions be sent to Botany Bay.

And that we may sweep our foul nation quite clean,
Send off the shop-tax promoters so mean,
And those who deprive the light of the day,
Should work for a breakfast at Botany Bay.

The hulks and the jails had some thousands in store,
But out of the jails are ten thousand times more,
Who live by fraud, cheating, vile tricks, and foul
     play,
They should all be sent over to Botany Bay.

Now, should any take umbrage, at what I have writ,
Or here find a bonnet or cap that will fit,
To such I have only this one word to say,
They are all welcome to wear it at Botany Bay.

                                        ANON

8

ROUGH WAGONS
ONE BY ONE

From **The Old Station**

IN 1861 the Legislature threw open all leasehold lands to the public for purchase on easy terms and conditions. The idea was to settle an industrious peasantry on lands hitherto leased in large blocks to the squatters. This brought down a flood of settlement on Kuryong. At the top end of the station there was a chain of mountains, and the country was rugged and patchy—rich valleys alternating with ragged hills. Here and there about the run were little patches of specially good land, which were soon snapped up. The pioneers of these small settlers were old Morgan Donohoe and his wife, who had built the hotel at Kiley's Crossing; and, on their reports, all their friends and relatives, as they came out of the "ould country", worked their way to Kuryong, and built little bits of slab and bark homesteads in among the mountains. The rougher the country, the better they liked it. They were a horse-thieving, sheep-stealing breed, and the talents which had made them poachers in the old country soon made them champion bushmen in their new surroundings. The leader of these mountain settlers was one Doyle, a gigantic Irishman, who had got a grant of a few hundred acres in the mountains, and had taken to himself a Scotch wife from among the free immigrants. The story ran that he was too busy to go to town, but asked a friend to go and pick a wife for him, "a fine shtrappin' woman, wid a good brisket on her".

The Doyles were large, slow, heavy men, with an instinct for the management of cattle; they were easily distinguished from the Donohoes, who were little red-whiskered men, enterprising and quick-witted, and ready to do anything in the world for a good horse. Other strangers and outlanders came to settle in the district, but from the original settlement up to the date of our story the two great families of the Doyles and the Donohoes governed the neighbourhood, and the headquarters of the clans was at Donohoe's "Shamrock Hotel", at Kiley's Crossing. Here they used to *rendezvous* when they went down to the plains country each year for the shearing; for they added to their resources by travelling about the country shearing, droving, fencing, tank-sinking, or doing any other job that offered itself, but always returned to their mountain fastnesses ready for any bit of work "on the cross" (i.e., unlawful) that might turn up. When

times got hard they had a handy knack of finding horses that nobody had lost, shearing sheep they did not own, and branding and selling other people's calves.

When they stole stock, they moved them on through the mountains as quickly as possible, always having a brother or uncle, or a cousin— Terry or Timothy or Martin or Patsy—who had a holding "beyant". By these means they could shift stolen stock across the great range, and dispose of them among the peaceable folk who dwelt in the good country on the other side, whose stock they stole in return. Many a good horse and fat beast had made the stealthy mountain journey, lying hidden in gaps and gullies when pursuit grew hot, and being moved on as things quieted down.

Another striking feature was the way in which they got themselves mixed up with each other. Their names were so tangled up that no one could keep tally of them. There was a Red Mick Donohoe (son of the old publican), and his cousin Black Mick Donohoe, and Red Mick's son Mick, and Black Mick's son Mick, and Red Mick's son Pat, and Black Mick's son Pat; and there was Gammy Doyle (meaning Doyle with the lame leg), and Scrammy Doyle (meaning Doyle with the injured arm), and Bosthoon Doyle and Omadhaun Doyle—a Bosthoon being a man who never had any great amount of sense to speak of, while an Omadhaun is a man who began life with some sense, but lost most of it on his journey. It was a common saying in the country-side that if you met a man on the mountains you should say, "Good-day, Doyle," and if he replied, "That's not my name," you should at once say, "Well, I meant no offence, Mr Donohoe."

One could generally pick which was which of the original stock, but when they came to intermarry there was no telling t'other from which. Startling likenesses cropped up among the relatives, and it was widely rumoured that one Doyle who was known to be in jail, and who was vaguely spoken of by the clan as being "away", was in fact serving an accumulation of sentences for himself and other members of the family, whose sins he had for a consideration taken on himself.

A. B. ("Banjo") PATERSON

Stringy-bark and Green-hide

 SING of a commodity, it's one that will not fail yer,
I mean that common oddity, the mainstay of Australia;
Gold it is a precious thing, for commerce it increases,
But stringy-bark and green-hide, can beat it all to
   pieces.

Chorus:
Stringy-bark and green-hide, they will never fail yer!
Stringy-bark and green-hide are the mainstay of Australia!

If you travel on the road, and chance to stick in Bargo,
To avoid a bad capsize, you must unload your cargo;
For to pull your dray about, I do not see the force on,
Take a bit of green-hide, and hook another horse on.

If you chance to take a dray, and break your leader's traces,
Get a bit of green-hide, to mend your broken places;
Green-hide is a useful thing, all that you require,
But stringy-bark's another thing when you want a fire.

If you want to build a hut, to keep out wind and weather,
Stringy-bark will make it snug, and keep it well together;
Green-hide if it's used by you, will make it all the stronger,
For if you tie it with green-hide, it's sure to last the longer.

New chums to this golden land, never dream of failure,
Whilst you've got such useful things as these in fair Australia.
For stringy-bark and green-hide will never, never fail yer,
Stringy-bark and green-hide are the mainstay of Australia.

ANON

It's Grand

IT'S grand to be a squatter
  And sit upon a post,
And watch your little ewes and lambs
  A-giving up the ghost.

It's grand to be a "cockie"
  With wife and kids to keep,
And find an all-wise Providence
  Has mustered all your sheep.

It's grand to be a Western man,
  With shovel in your hand,
To dig your little homestead out
  From underneath the sand.

It's grand to be a shearer
  Along the Darling-side,
And pluck the wool from stinking sheep
  That some days since have died.

.   .   .   .   .   .

It's grand to be a lot of things
  In this fair Southern land,
But if the Lord would send us rain,
  That would, indeed, be grand!

A. B. ("Banjo") PATERSON

From **The Old Bark School**

IT was built of bark and poles, and the roof was full
    of holes
  And each leak in rainy weather made a pool;
And the walls were mostly cracks lined with calico
    and sacks—
  There was little need for windows in the school.

Then we rode to school and back by the rugged
    gully-track,
  On the old grey horse that carried three or four;
And he looked so very wise that he lit the Master's
    eyes
  Every time he put his head in at the door.

.   .   .   .   .   .

And we learnt the world in scraps from some ancient
    dingy maps
  Long discarded by the public-schools in town;
And as nearly every book dated back to Captain
    Cook
  Our geography was somewhat upside-down.

.   .   .   .   .   .

Now the old bark school is gone, and the spot it
    stood upon
  Is a cattle-camp where curlews' cries are heard;
There's a brick school on the flat—an old school-mate
    teaches that—
  It was built when Mr Kevin was "transferred".

HENRY LAWSON

Squatter's Song

HURRAH! for the damper, the beef and the tin,
The little black pipe and the little black gin;
With our sheep and our horses, our cattle and goats,
Our breeches of leather and Wallaby coats.

Hurrah! for our log-huts, so snug in retreat,
When strangers the squatter hospitably meet,
It's off with your saddle and hobble your horse,
With salt beef and damper there's never a choice.

Alas! these new taxes may make us to pause
And give no relief e'en in poverty's cause.
Then down with the taxes; rise freedom and ease
Sir George from his charge which will ever displease.

June the first on the Hill a trial we'll have,
Our cheers shall cause Batman to peep from his
     grave;
He'll nod his assent, he'll spur us along,
There's nought to oppose us of 1000 strong.

The troopers may come with their carbines and
     swords,
The Super may blarney with his soapy words;
But we of the tin and the damper will die
Round our standard for freedom—Sir George mind
     your eye!

ANON

From **Middleton's Peter**

A T last, far out through the trunks of the native apple-trees, the cart was seen approaching; and as it came nearer it was evident that it was being driven at a breakneck pace, the horses cantering all the way, while the motion of the cart, as first one wheel and then the other sprang from a root or a rut, bore a striking resemblance to the Highland Fling. There were two persons in the cart. One was Mother Palmer, a stout, middle-aged party (who sometimes did the duties of a midwife), and the other was Dave Middleton, Joe's brother.

The cart was driven right up to the door with scarcely any abatement of speed, and was stopped so suddenly that Mrs Palmer was sent sprawling on to the horse's rump. She was quickly helped down, and, as soon as she had recovered sufficient breath, she followed Black Mary into the bedroom where young Mrs Middleton was lying, looking very pale and frightened. The horse which had been driven so cruelly had not done blowing before another cart appeared, also driven very fast. It contained old Mr and Mrs Middleton, who lived comfortably on a small farm not far from Palmer's place.

As soon as he had dumped Mrs Palmer, Dave Middleton left the cart and, mounting a fresh horse which stood ready saddled in the yard, galloped off through the scrub in a different direction.

Half an hour afterwards Joe Middleton came home on a horse that had been almost ridden to death. His mother came out at the sound of his arrival, and he anxiously asked her:

"How is she?"

"Did you find Doc Wild?" asked the mother.

"No, confound him!" exclaimed Joe bitterly. "He promised me faithfully to come over on Wednesday and stay until Maggie was right again. Now he has left Dean's and gone—Lord knows where. I suppose he is drinking again. How is Maggie?"

"It's all over now—the child is born. It's a boy; but she is very weak. Dave got Mrs Palmer here just in time. I had better tell you at once that Mrs Palmer says if we don't get a doctor here to-night poor Maggie won't live."

HENRY LAWSON

The Women of the West

THEY left the vine-wreathed cottage and the mansion on
   the hill,
The houses in the busy streets where life is never still,
The pleasures of the city, and the friends they cherished
   best:
For love they faced the wilderness—the Women of the
   West.

The roar, and rush, and fever of the city died away,
And the old-time joys and faces—they were gone for many a day;
In their place the lurching coach-wheel, or the creaking bullock
   chains,
O'er the everlasting sameness of the never-ending plains.

In the slab-built, zinc-roofed homestead of some lately-taken run,
In the tent beside the bankment of a railway just begun,
In the huts on new selections, in the camps of man's unrest,
On the frontiers of the Nation, live the Women of the West.

The red sun robs their beauty, and, in weariness and pain,
The slow years steal the nameless grace that never comes again;
And there are hours men cannot soothe, and words men cannot
   say—
The nearest woman's face may be a hundred miles away.

The wide Bush holds the secrets of their longings and desires,
When the white stars in reverence light their holy altar-fires,
And silence, like the touch of God, sinks deep into the breast—
Perchance He hears and understands the Women of the West.

For them no trumpet sounds the call, no poet plies his arts—
They only hear the beating of their gallant, loving hearts.
But they have sung with silent lives the song all songs above—
The holiness of sacrifice, the dignity of love.

Well have we held our father's creed. No call has passed us by.
We faced and fought the wilderness, we sent our sons to die.
And we have hearts to do and dare, and yet, o'er all the rest,
The hearts that made the Nation were the Women of the West.

GEORGE ESSEX EVANS

GULGONG, GRIEF AND GOLD

An Old Mate Of Your Father's

YOU remember when we hurried home from the old bush school how we were sometimes startled by a bearded apparition, who smiled kindly down on us, and whom our mother introduced, as we raked off our hats, as "An old mate of your father's on the diggings, Johnny." And he would pat our heads and say we were fine boys, or girls—as the case may have been—and that we had our father's nose but our mother's eyes, or the other way about; and say that the baby was the dead spit of its mother, and then added, for father's benefit: "But yet he's like you, Tom." It did seem strange to the children to hear him address the old man by his Christian name—considering that the mother always referred to him as "Father". She called the old mate Mr So-and-so, and father called him Bill, or something to that effect.

Occasionally the old mate would come dressed in the latest city fashion, and at other times in a new suit of reach-me-downs, and yet again he would turn up in clean white moleskins, washed tweed coat, Crimean shirt, blucher boots, soft felt hat, with a fresh-looking speckled handkerchief round his neck. But his face was mostly round and brown and jolly, his hands were always horny, and his beard grey. Sometimes he might have seemed strange and uncouth to us at first, but the old man never appeared the least surprised at anything he said or did—they understood each other so well—and we would soon take to this relic of our father's past, who would have fruit or lollies for us—strange that he always remembered them—and would surreptitiously slip "shilluns" into our dirty little hands, and tell us stories about the old days, "when me an' yer father was on the diggin's, an' you wasn't thought of, my boy".

Sometimes the old mate would stay over Sunday, and

in the forenoon or after dinner he and father would take a walk amongst the deserted shafts of Sapling Gully or along Quartz Ridge, and criticize old ground, and talk of past diggers' mistakes, and second bottoms, and feelers, and dips, and leads—also outcrops—and absently pick up pieces of quartz and slate, rub them on their sleeves, look at them in an abstracted manner, and drop them again; and they would talk of some old lead they had worked on: "Hogan's party was here on one side of us, Macintosh was here on the other, Mac was getting good gold and so was Hogan, and now, why the blanky blank weren't we on gold?" And the mate would always agree that there was "gold in them ridges and gullies yet, if a man only had the money behind him to git at it". And then perhaps the guv'nor would show him a spot where he intended to put down a shaft some day— the old man was always thinking of putting down a shaft. And these two old fifty-niners would mooch round and sit on their heels on the sunny mullock heaps and break clay lumps between their hands, and lay plans for the putting down of shafts, and smoke, till an urchin was sent to "look for your father and Mr So-and-so, and tell 'em to come to their dinner."

And again—mostly in the fresh of the morning— they would hang about the fences on the selection and review the live stock: five dusty skeletons of cows, a hollow-sided calf or two, and one shocking piece of equine scenery—which, by the way, the old mate always praised. But the selector's heart was not in farming nor on selections—it was far away with the last new rush in Western Australia or Queensland, or perhaps buried in the worked-out ground of Tambaroora, Married Man's Creek, or Araluen; and by and by the memory of some half-forgotten reef or lead or Last Chance, Nil Desperandum, or Brown Snake claim would take their thoughts far back and away from the dusty patch of sods and struggling sprouts called the crop, or the few discouraged, half-dead slips which comprised the orchard. Then their conversation would be pointed with many Golden Points, Bakery Hills, Deep Creeks, Maitland Bars, Specimen Flats, and Chinamen's Gullies. And so they'd yarn till the youngster came to tell them that "Mother sez the breakfus is gettin' cold," and then the old mate would rouse himself and stretch and say, "Well, we mustn't keep the missus waitin', Tom!"

And, after tea, they would sit on a log of the wood-heap, or the edge of the veranda—that is, in warm weather—and yarn about Ballarat and Bendigo—of the days when we spoke of being on a place oftener than at it: *on* Ballarat, *on* Gulgong, *on* Lambing Flat, *on* Creswick—and they would use the definite article before the names, as: "on The Turon; The Lachlan; The Home Rule; The Canadian Lead." Then again they'd yarn of old mates, such as Tom Brook, Jack Henright, and poor Martin Ratcliffe—who was killed in his golden hole—and of other men whom they didn't seem to have known much about, and who went by the names of "Adelaide Adolphus", "Corney George", and other names which might have been more or less applicable.

And sometimes they'd get talking, low and mysterious like, about "Th' Eureka Stockade"; and if we didn't understand and asked questions, "what was the Eureka Stockade?" or "what did they do it for?" father'd say: "Now, run away, sonny, an don't bother; me and Mr So-and-so want to talk." Father had the mark of a hole on his leg, which he said he got through a gun accident when a boy, and a scar on his side, that we saw when he was in swimming with us; he said he got that in an accident in a quartz-crushing machine. Mr So-and-so had a big scar on the side of his forehead that was caused by a pick accidentally slipping out of a loop in the rope, and falling down a shaft where he was working. But how was it they talked low, and their eyes brightened up, and they didn't look at each other, but away over the sunset, and had to get up and walk about, and take a stroll in the cool of the evening when

they talked about Eureka?

And, again they'd talk lower and more mysterious like, and perhaps mother would be passing the wood-heap and catch a word, and ask:

"Who was she, Tom?"

And Tom—father—would say:

"Oh, you didn't know her, Mary; she belonged to a family Bill knew at home."

And Bill would look solemn till mother had gone, and then they would smile a quiet smile, and stretch and say, "Ah, well!" and start something else.

They had yarns for the fireside, too, some of those old mates of our father's, and one of them would often tell how a girl—a queen of the diggings—was married, and had her wedding-ring made out of the gold of that field; and how the diggers weighed their gold with the new wedding-ring—for luck—by hanging the ring on the hook of the scales and attaching their chamois-leather gold bags to it (whereupon she boasted that four hundred ounces of the precious metal passed through her wedding-ring); and how they lowered the young bride, blindfolded, down a golden hole in a big bucket, and got her to point out the drive from which the gold came that her ring was made out of. The point of this story seems to have been lost—or else we forget it—but it was characteristic. Had the girl been lowered down a duffer, and asked to point out the way to the gold, and had she done so successfully, there would have been some sense in it.

And they would talk of King, and Maggie Oliver, and G. V. Brooke, and others, and remember how the diggers went five miles out to meet the coach that brought the girl actress, and took the horses out and brought her in in triumph, and worshipped her, and sent her off in glory, and threw nuggets into her lap. And how she stood upon the box-seat and tore her sailor hat to pieces, and threw the fragments amongst the crowd; and how the diggers fought for the bits and thrust them inside their shirt bosoms; and how she broke down and cried, and could in her turn have worshipped those men—loved them, every one. They were boys all, and gentlemen all. There were college men, artists, poets, musicians, journalists—Bohemians all. Men from all the lands and one. They understood art—and poverty was dead.

And perhaps the old mate would say slyly, but with a sad, quiet smile:

"Have you got that bit of straw yet, Tom?"

Those old mates had each three pasts behind them. The two they told each other when they became mates, and the one they had shared.

And when the visitor had gone by the coach we noticed that the old man would smoke a lot, and think as much, and take great interest in the fire, and be a trifle irritable perhaps.

Those old mates of our father's are getting few and far between, and only happen along once in a way to keep the old man's memory fresh, as it were. We met one to-day, and had a yarn with him, and afterwards we got thinking, and somehow began to wonder whether those ancient friends of ours were, or were not, better and kinder to their mates than we of the rising generation are to our fathers; and the doubt is painfully on the wrong side.

HENRY LAWSON

From **The Roaring Days**

T HE night too quickly passes
 And we are growing old,
So let us fill our glasses
 And toast the Days of Gold;
When finds of wondrous treasure
 Set all the South ablaze,
And you and I were faithful mates
All through the roaring days!

Then stately ships came sailing
 From every harbour's mouth,
And sought the land of promise
 That beaconed in the South;
Then southward streamed their streamers
 And swelled their canvas full
To speed the wildest dreamers
 E'er borne in vessel's hull.

Their shining Eldorado,
 Beneath the southern skies,
Was day and night for ever
 Before their eager eyes.
The brooding bush, awakened,
 Was stirred in wild unrest,
And all the year a human stream
 Went pouring to the West.

.   .   .   .   .

Oh! who would paint a goldfield,
 And limn the picture right,
As old Adventure saw it
 In early morning's light?
The yellow mounds of mullock,
 With spots of red and white,
The scattered quartz that glistened,
 Like diamonds in light.

The azure line of ridges,
　The bush of darkest green,
The little homes of calico,
　That dotted all the scene,
The flat, straw hats with ribands.
　That old engravings show—
The dress that still reminds us,
　Of sailors long ago.

I hear the fall of timber,
　From distant flats and fells,
The pealing of the anvils,
　As clear as little bells,
The rattle of the cradle,
　The clack of windlass boles,
The flutter of the crimson flags,
　Above the golden holes.

Ah! then their hearts were bolder,
　And if Dame Fortune frowned,
Their swags they'd lightly shoulder,
　And tramp to other ground.
Oh! they were lion-hearted,
　Who gave our country birth,
Stout sons of stoutest fathers born,
　From all the lands of earth.

Those golden days have vanished,
　And altered is the scene;
The diggings are deserted,
　The camping-grounds are green;
The flaunting flag of progress
　Is in the West unfurled,
The mighty bush with iron rails
　Is tethered to the world.

HENRY LAWSON

From **The Loaded Dog**

"R UN, Andy! Run!'' they shouted back at him. "Run! Look behind you, you fool!'' Andy turned slowly and looked, and there, close behind him, was the retriever with the cartridge in his mouth—wedged into his broadest and silliest grin. And that wasn't all. The dog had come round the fire to Andy, and the loose end of the fuse had trailed and waggled over the burning sticks into the blaze; Andy had slit and nicked the firing end of the fuse well, and now it was hissing and spitting properly.

Andy's legs started with a jolt; his legs started before his brain did, and he made after Dave and Jim. And the dog followed Andy.

Dave and Jim were good runners—Jim the best—for a short distance; Andy was slow and heavy, but he had the strength and the wind and could last. The dog capered round him, delighted as a dog could be to find his mates, as he thought, on for a frolic. Dave and Jim kept shouting back, "Don't foller us! Don't foller us, you coloured fool!'' But Andy kept on, no matter how they dodged. They could never explain, any more than the dog, why they followed each other, but so they ran, Dave keeping in Jim's track in all its turnings, Andy after Dave, and the dog circling round Andy—the live fuse swishing in all directions and hissing and spluttering and stinking.

HENRY LAWSON

30

Percy Lindsay

"Have you a miner's right?"

I THEN returned to Erskine Flat to work at the scene of my first venture on the goldfield, and sank a hole near the first quarters I occupied.... My mates in this new venture were quite strangers to me. On bottoming we got a good show, and commenced breaking down and washing. The gold-bearing dirt here was of such a thickness that in tunnelling it out we had to lengthen our pick handles. I was at the cradle one day, and had just come up for a barrow of stuff, when who should suddenly ride up over the rise, followed by a trooper and a chain of handcuffed men, but Mr I—, clerk of the court, acting as I found for the Commissioner.

His first words were, "Have you a miner's right?" (then 30s. per month). I answered, "Yes." "Show it me." "It's down the hole in my waistcoat pocket." "Go and fetch it."

So, fastening the rope to the windlass-stand, I descended, crept into the tunnel, and whispered to my mate, "Lend me your miner's right." I got it and was ascending when a thought struck me—"If he asks my name, as I can't read and don't know my mate's name, I'll be in a fix." ... The first salute on top was, "What's your name?" I answered, "I sha'n't tell you my name, nor show my right; I don't believe from your dress you're a Commissioner, nor that you have any authority."

I was handcuffed and ordered on the chain, and after it had received a few additions we were marched back to the camp, about a mile and a-half off. There we were ranked up in front of the office, and out came the Commissioners, Messrs Johnstone and Maclean. Some were fined and had to pay the right, and others sent to the lockup.

When my turn came Mr I— said, "This man refused to give his name, or show his right." The Commissioner then repeated the question, and to get out of the trap, and avoid giving a direct answer, I said, "He doesn't look like a Commissioner, look at his hat" (not the uniform).

"Hat or no hat," said Mr Maclean, "if I send anyone round with authority to inspect rights, and I find you or anyone defy him, I'll give you the chain to some purpose, my bold 'Bill Day'." I thus, by the Commissioner's own words, found out my mate's name on the borrowed right, and wriggled out of the scrape. After that for years I went by that name.

WILLIAM DERRINCOURT (alias W. Day)

SOME ROGUES AND BUCCANEERS

The Wild Colonial Boy

'TIS of a wild Colonial boy, Jack Doolan was his name,
Of poor but honest parents he was born in Castlemaine.
He was his father's only hope, his mother's only joy,
And dearly did his parents love the wild Colonial boy.

Chorus:
Come, all my hearties, we'll roam the mountains high,
Together we will plunder, together we will die.
We'll wander over valleys, and gallop over plains,
And we'll scorn to live in slavery, bound down with iron chains.

He was scarcely sixteen years of age when he left his father's home,
And through Australia's sunny clime a bushranger did roam.
He robbed those wealthy squatters, their stock he did destroy,
And a terror to Australia was the wild Colonial boy.

In sixty-one this daring youth commenced his wild career,
With a heart that knew no danger, no foeman did he fear.
He stuck up the Beechworth mail-coach, and robbed Judge
  MacEvoy,
Who trembled, and gave up his gold to the wild Colonial boy.

He bade the judge "Good morning", and told him to beware,
That he'd never rob a hearty chap that acted on the square,
And never to rob a mother of her son and only joy,
Or else you may turn outlaw, like the wild Colonial boy.

One day as he was riding the mountain-side along,
A-listening to the little birds, their pleasant laughing song,
Three mounted troopers rode along—Kelly, Davis, and FitzRoy—
They thought that they would capture him, the wild Colonial boy.

"Surrender now, Jack Doolan, you see there's three to one.
Surrender now, Jack Doolan, you daring highwayman."
He drew a pistol from his belt, and shook the little toy.
"I'll fight, but not surrender," said the wild Colonial boy.

He fired at Trooper Kelly and brought him to the ground,
And in return from Davis received a mortal wound.
All shattered through the jaws he lay still firing at FitzRoy,
And that's the way they captured him—the wild Colonial boy.

ANON

Ballad of Jack Lefroy

COME all you lads and listen, a story I would tell,
Before they take me out and hang me high;
My name is Jack Lefroy, and life I would enjoy,
But the old judge has sentenced me to die.
My mother she was Irish and she taught me at her
    knee,
But to steady work I never did incline,
As a youngster I could ride any horse was wrapped in hide,
And when I saw a good 'un he was mine.

Chorus:
So all young lads take warning and don't be led astray,
For the past you never, never can recall;
While young your gifts employ, take a lesson from Lefroy,
Let fate be a warning to you all.

Go straight, young man, they told me when my first long stretch
    was done;
If you're jugg'd again you'll have yourself to thank;
But I swore I'd not be found hunting nuggets in the ground
When the biggest could be picked up in the bank.
Well, I've stuck up some mail coaches, and I've ridden with Ben
    Hall,
And they never got me cornered once until
A pimp was in their pay —gave my dingo hole away,
And they run me to earth at Riley's Hill.

"Come out, Lefroy!" they called me: "Come out, we're five to
    one;"
But I took my pistols out and stood my ground.
For an hour I pumped out lead till they got me in the head,
And when I awoke they had me bound.
It's a pleasant day to live, boys, a gloomy one to die,
A dangling with your neck inside a string,
How I'd like to ride again down the hills to Lachlan Plain!
But when the sun rises I must swing.

ANON

The Morning of the Fray

"COME on, boys," says the Darkie, with the devil in
  his eye;
"Come, blacken up: get ready: for ere the fall o'
  night,
We've merry work before us—we've got to do or
  die;
At Eugowra rocks ere sundown, we've got to fall or
  fight.
We'll stop the Orange escort with powder and with
  ball,
Lift the diggers' money, and collar all the gold,
Smash the coach to pieces, and down the peelers all—
So mind your guns are killers, my comrades, brave
  and bold:
There's only four policemen and ten of us all told."

Bang! bang! go off the rifles: the battle has begun;
Ah! see the escort running; and now the robbers bold
Seize upon the plunder, and with the setting sun
They're riding from Eugowra encumbered with the
  gold;
And as with savage laughter they leave the fated
  place,
Gardiner—that's "the Darkie"—is shouting loud,
  "Hooray!
Hooray; we've struck Bonanza; we've won the
  steeplechase—
I think we've made our fortunes at Eugowra rocks
  today."
And so with wicked jesting the outlaws rode away.

FRANK GARDINER (?)

The Style in Which It's Done

FRIEND Draper steals ten thousand pounds,
And gets three years in gaol;
While Devil Dick gets seventeen
For sticking up the mail.
One punishment is over
When the other's just begun,
Which shows how much depends upon
The style in which it's done.

ANON

THE TEAMSTERS,
DROVERS, SWAGMEN

The Champion Bullock-Driver

WE were sitting outside old Tallwood cattle-station, in our white moleskin trousers, elastic-side boots, and cabbage-tree hats, watching two stockmen shoe a very wild brumby mare. We were all slaves to the saddle and bridle, and there was nothing too heavy or hard. The boss squatted on a new four-rail fence. There were twenty panels of this fence, strong iron bark post-and-rails. The first rails were mortised into a big iron-bark tree, and there were four No. 8 wires twisted around the butt, passed through the posts and strained very tightly to the big strainer at the other end.

As though he had dropped out of the sky there appeared on the scene a very smart-looking man carrying a red-blanket swag, a water-bag, tucker-bag, and billy-can. He put them down and said, "Is the boss about?"

We all pointed to the man on the fence. The new chap took his pipe out of his mouth and walked up, a bit shy-like, and said,

"Is there any chance of a job, boss?"

"What can you do?" asked the boss.

"Well, anything amongst stock. You can't put me wrong."

"Can you ride a buckjumper?"

"Pretty good," said the young man.

"Can you scrub-dash—I mean, can you catch cattle in timber on a good horse before they're knocked up?"

"Hold my own," said the young man.

"Have you got a good flow of language?"

The young man hesitated awhile before answering this question. So the boss said,

"I mean, can you drive a rowdy team of bullocks?"

"Just into my hand," said the young man.

The boss jumped down off the fence.

"Look here," he said, "It's no good you telling me you can drive a team of bullocks if you can't."

And pointing to a little grave-yard he added,

"Do you see that little cemetery over there?"

The young man pulled his hat down over his eye, looked across, and said, "Yes."

"Well," continued the boss, "there are sixteen bullock-drivers lying there. They came here to drive this team of mine."

I watched the young man's face when the boss said that to see if he would flinch; but a little smile broke away from the corner of his mouth, curled around his cheek and disappeared in his earhole, and as the effect died away he said,

"They won't put me there."

"I don't know so much about that," said the boss.

"I'll give you a trial," the young man suggested.

"It would take too long to muster the bullocks," said the boss. "But take that bullock-whip there"—it was standing near the big ironbark—"and say, for instance, eight panels of that fence are sixteen bullocks, show me how you would start up the team."

"Right," said the young man.

Walking over he picked up the big bullock-whip and very carefully examined it to see how it was fastened to the handle. Then he ran his hand down along the whip, examining it as though he were searching for a broken link in a chain. Then he looked closely to see how the fall was fastened to the whip. After that he stood back and swung it around and gave a cheer.

First he threw the whip up to the leaders, and then threw it back to the polers. He stepped in as though to dig the near-side pin-bullock under the arm with the handle of the whip, then stepped back and swung the big bullock around. He kept on talking, and the whip kept on cracking, until a little flame ran right along the top of the fence. And he kept on talking and the whip kept on cracking until the phantom forms of sixteen bullocks appeared along the fence—blues, blacks and brindles. And he kept on talking and the whip kept on cracking till the phantom forms of sixteen bullock-drivers appeared on the scene. And they kept on talking and their whips kept on cracking till the fence started to walk on, and pulled the big ironbark tree down.

"That will do," said the boss.

"Not a bit of it," said the young man, "where's your woodheap?"

We all pointed to the woodheap near the old bark kitchen.

And they kept on talking and their whips kept on cracking till they made the fence pull the tree right up to the woodheap.

We were all sitting round on the limbs of the tree, and the young man was talking to the boss, and we felt sure he would get the job, when the boss called out,

"Get the fencing-gear lads, and put that fence up again."

"Excuse me for interrupting, boss," said the young man, "but would you like to see how I back a team of bullocks?"

"Yes, I would," said the boss.

So the young man walked over and picked up the big bullock-whip again. He swung it around and called out,

"Now then, boys, all together!"

And the phantom forms of the sixteen bullock-drivers appeared on the scene again; and they kept on talking and their whips kept on cracking, till every post and rail burst out into flame, and when the flame cleared away each post and rail backed into its place, and the phantom forms of the sixteen bullock-drivers saluted the young man, then bowed and backed, and bowed and backed right into their graves, recognising him as the champion bullock-driver.

LANCE SKUTHORPE

Five Miles from Gundagai

I'M used to punchin' bullock-teams
  Across the hills and plains,
I've teamed outback this forty years
  In blazin' droughts and rains,
I've lived a heap of trouble down
  Without a bloomin' lie,
But I can't forget what happened to me
  Five miles from Gundagai.

'Twas gettin' dark, the team got bogged,
  The axle snapped in two;
I lost me matches an' me pipe,
  So what was I to do?
The rain came on, 'twas bitter cold,
  And hungry too was I,
And the dog he sat in the tucker-box,
  Five miles from Gundagai.

Some blokes I know has stacks o' luck,
  No matter 'ow they fall,
But there was I, Lord love a duck!
  No blasted luck at all.
I couldn't make a pot o' tea,
  Nor get me trousers dry,
And the dog sat in the tucker-box,
  Five miles from Gundagai.

I can forgive the blinkin' team,
  I can forgive the rain,
I can forgive the dark and cold,
  And go through it again,
I can forgive me rotten luck,
  But hang me till I die,
I can't forgive that bloody dog
  Five miles from Gundagai.

ANON

A Droving Yarn

NDY MACULLOCH had heard that old Bill Barker, the well-known overland drover, had died over on the Westralian side, and Dave Regan told a yarn about Bill.

"Bill Barker," said Dave, talking round his pipe stem, "was the *quintessence* of a drover—"

"The whatter, Dave?" came the voice of Jim Bently, in startled tones, from the gloom on the far end of the veranda.

"The quintessence," said Dave, taking his pipe out of his mouth. "You shut up, Jim. As I said, Bill Barker was the quintessence of a drover. He'd been at the game ever since he was a nipper. He ran away from home when he was fourteen and went up into Queensland. He's been all over Queensland and New South Wales and most of South Australia, and a good deal of the Western, too: over the great stock routes from one end to the other, Lord knows how many times. No man could keep up with him riding out, and no one could bring a mob of cattle or a flock of sheep through like him. He knew every trick of the game; if there was grass to be had Bill'd get it, no matter whose run it was on. One of his games in a dry season was to let his mob get boxed with the station stock on a run where there was grass, and before Bill's men and the station-hands could cut 'em out, the travelling stock would have a good bellyful to carry them on the track. Billy was the daddy of the drovers. Some said that he could ride in his sleep, and that he had one old horse that could jog along in his sleep, too, and that—travelling out from home to take charge of a mob of bullocks or a flock of sheep—Bill and his horse would often wake up at daylight and blink round to see where they were and how far they'd got. Then Bill would make a fire and boil his quart-pot, and roast a bit of mutton, while his horse had a mouthful of grass and a spell.

"You remember Bill, Andy? Big dark man, and a joker of the loud sort. Never slept with a blanket over him—always folded under him on the sand or grass. Seldom wore a coat on the route—though he always carried one with him, in case he came across a bush ball or a funeral. Moleskins, flannel waistcoat, cabbage-tree hat and 'lastic-side boots. When it was roasting hot on the plains and the men swore at the heat, Bill would yell, 'Call this hot? Why, you blanks, I'm freezin'! Where's me overcoat?' When it was raining and hailing and freezing on Bell's

Line in the Blue Mountains in winter, and someone shivered and asked, 'Is it cold enough for yer now, Bill?' 'Cold!' Bill would bellow, 'I'm sweatin'!'

"I remember it well. I was little more than a youngster then—Bill Barker came past our place with about a thousand fat sheep for the Homebush sale-yards at Sydney, and he gave me a job to help him down with them on Bell's Line over the mountains, and mighty proud I was to go with him, I can tell you. One night we camped on the Cudge-gong River. The country was dry and pretty close cropped and we'd been 'sweating' the paddocks all along there for our horses. You see, where there weren't sliprails handy we'd just take the tomahawk and nick the top of a straight-grained fence-post, just above the mortise, knock out the wood there, lift the top rail out and down, and jump the horses in over the lower one—it was all two-rail fences around there with sheep wires under the lower rail. And about daylight we'd have the horses out, lift back the rail, and fit in the chock that we'd knocked out. Simple as striking matches, wasn't it?

"Well, the horses were getting a good bellyful in the police horse paddock at night, and Bill took the first watch with the sheep. It was very cold and frosty on the flat and he thought the sheep might make back for the ridges, it's always warmer up in the ridges in winter out of the frost. Bill roused me out about midnight. 'There's the sheep,' he says, pointing to a white blur. 'They've settled down. I think they'll be quiet till daylight. Don't go round them; there's no occasion to go near 'em. You can stop by the fire and keep an eye on 'em.'

"The night seemed very long. I watched and smoked and toasted my shins, and warmed the billy now and then, and thought up pretty much the same sort of old things that fellers on night watch think over all over the world. Bill lay on his blanket, with his back to the fire and his arm under his head—freezing on one side and roasting on the other. He never moved—I itched once or twice to turn him over and bake the front of him—I reckoned he was about done behind.

"At last daylight showed. I took the billy and started down to the river to get some water to make coffee; but half-way down, near the sheep camp, I stopped and stared, I was never so surprised in my life. The white blur of sheep had developed into a couple of acres of long dead silver grass!

"I woke Bill, and he swore as I never heard a man swear before—nor since. He swore at the sheep, and the grass, and at me;

but it would have wasted time, and besides I was too sleepy and tired to fight. But we found those sheep scattered over a scrubby ridge about seven miles back, so they must have slipped away back of the grass and started early in Bill's watch, and Bill must have watched that blessed grass for the first half of the night and then set me to watch it. He couldn't get away from that.

"I wondered what the chaps would say if it got round that Bill Barker, the boss overland drover, had lost a thousand sheep in clear country with fences all round; and I suppose he thought that way too, for he kept me with him right down to Homebush, and when he paid me off he threw in an extra quid, and he said:

"'Now, listen here, Dave! If I ever hear a word from anyone about watching that gory grass, I'll find you, Dave, and murder you, if you're in wide Australia. I'll screw your neck, so look out.'

"But he's dead now, so it doesn't matter."

There was silence for some time after Dave had finished. The chaps made no comment on the yarn, either one way or the other, but sat smoking thoughtfully, and in a vague atmosphere as of sadness—as if they'd just heard of their mother's death and had not been listening to an allegedly humorous yarn.

Then the voice of old Peter, the station-hand, was heard to growl from the darkness at the end of the hut, where he sat on a three-bushel bag on the ground with his back to the slabs.

"What's old Peter growlin' about?" someone asked.

"He wants to know where Dave got that word," someone else replied.

"What word?"

"*Quint-essents.*"

There was a chuckle.

"He got it out back, Peter," said Mitchell, the shearer. "He got it from a new chum."

"How much did yer give for it, Dave?" growled Peter.

"Five shillings, Peter," said Dave, round his pipe stem. "And stick of tobacco thrown in."

Peter seemed satisfied, for he was heard no more that evening.

HENRY LAWSON

The Flash Stockman

I'M a stockman to my trade, and they call me ugly Dave;
I'm old and grey and only got one eye.
In a yard I'm good, of course, but just put me on a
    horse,
And I'll go where lots of young 'uns daren't try.

I lead 'em through the gidgee over country rough and ridgy.
I lose 'em in the very worst of scrub;
I can ride both rough and easy, with a dewdrop I'm a daisy,
And a right-down bobby-dazzler in a pub.

Just watch me use a whip, I can give the dawdlers gyp,
I can make the bloody echoes roar and ring;
With a branding-iron, well, I'm a perfect flaming swell,
In fact, I'm duke of every blasted thing.

To watch me skin a sheep, it's so lovely you could weep;
I can act the silvertail as if my blood was blue;
You can strike me pink or dead, if I stood upon my head,
I'd be just as good as any other two.

I've a notion in my pate, that it's luck, it isn't fate,
That I'm so far above the common run;
So in every thing I do, you could cut me fair in two,
For I'm much too bloody good to be in one!

ANON

49

The Outlaw and the Rider

H E had come to Umarella when the drought of '98
Had made Monara Plains a sea of sand,
And the philanthropic super, taking pity on his state,
Had given him a start as extra hand.

No doubt he'd been a wonder, for at night he'd sit for
hours,
And boast of marvellous feats he'd seen and done,
How he'd won the Axeman's Trophy at the Show in Charters
Towers,
And had killed a Syrian hawker just for fun.

How he rung the shed at Blackall, beating Howe by thirty sheep,
He'd broken outlaw horses in at night,
And in seven rounds at Gympie put O'Sullivan to sleep
With a blow for which he had the patent right.

Now we had a horse, an outlaw, bred on Umarella run,
No fiercer colt had ever stretched the reins,
He had thrown Monara Billy and the station breaker, Dunne,
And was reckoned bad throughout the southern plains.

The Skipper came down strolling—we had planned the joke of
course—
"I've letters here, must catch the mail," he said;
"You had better take them, Jimmy, you can ride the chestnut
horse,
But mind him or he'll have you on your head."

Now, Jim threw on the saddle and the colt stood like a sheep
One moment and we thought our joke would fail,
But Jim was barely seated when the colt he gave a leap,
And went at it like a demon through the rails.

Down the lane we followed and we opened wide our eyes
To see Jim like a perfect horseman sit,
He would fetch the stockwhip round him every time the colt
    would rise
And would tease him with the spurs whene'er he lit.

We made a rush for horses, down the lane we followed fast,
To see our outlaw thrashed was something new,
But when we reached the clump of trees where we had seen him
    last,
Both horse and man had disappeared from view.

For miles the track we followed, and for days we sought in vain,
All was bustle, horsemen riding here and there,
From the cattle camp on Kindra to the farms on Little Plain,
We searched the rugged country in despair.

The days to weeks had lengthened, still no tidings came to hand,
We felt all hope of finding them was lost,
Till a party searching eastward saw some footprints in the sand,
Showing plainly that a horse had lately crossed.

So we tracked along the hoof-marks where once deep grasses grew,
And on a flat hemmed in by gorges deep
We found that chestnut bucking still for all he ever knew,
And Jim was there astride him, fast asleep.

ANON

From Who's Riding Old Harlequin Now?

THEY are mustering cattle on Brigalow Vale
Where the stock-horses whinny and stamp,
And where long Andy Ferguson, you may go bail,
Is yet boss on a cutting-out camp.
Half the duffers I met would not know a fat steer
From a blessed old Alderney cow;
Whilst they're mustering there I am wondering
     here—
Who is riding brown Harlequin now?

Are the pikers as wild and the scrubs just as dense
In the brigalow country as when
There was never a homestead and never a fence
Between Brigalow Vale and The Glen?
Do they yard the big micks 'neath the light of the
     moon?
Do the yard-wings re-echo the row
Of stockwhips and hoof-beats? And what sort of
     coon
Is there riding old Harlequin now?

There was buckjumping blood in the brown
     gelding's veins,
But, lean-headed, with iron-like pins,
Of Pyrrhus and Panic he'd plentiful strains,
All their virtues, and some of their sins.
'Twas pity, some said, that so shapely a colt
Fate should with such temper endow;
He would kick and would strike, he would buck and
     would bolt—
Ah! who's riding brown Harlequin now?

A demon to handle! a devil to ride!
Small wonder the surcingle burst;
You'd have thought that he'd buck himself out of
   his hide
On the morning we saddled him first.
I can mind how he cow-kicked the spur on my boot,
And though that's long ago, still I vow
If they're wheeling a piker no new-chum galoot
Is a-riding old Harlequin now!

I remember the boss—how he chuckled and laughed
When they yarded the brown colt for me:
"He'll be steady enough when we finish the graft
And have cleaned up the scrubs of Glen Leigh!"
I am wondering today if the brown horse yet live,
For the fellow who broke him, I trow,
A long lease of soul-ease would willingly give
To be riding brown Harlequin now!

HARRY MORANT
("The Breaker")

A Snake Yarn

"YOU talk of snakes," said Jack the Rat,
"But, blow me, one hot summer,
I seen a thing that knocked me flat—
Fourteen foot long, or more than that,
It was a regular hummer!
Lay right along a sort of bog,
  Just like a log!

"The ugly thing was lyin' there
And not a sign o' movin',
Give any man a nasty scare;
Seen nothin' like it anywhere
Since I first started drovin'.
And yet it didn't scare my dog.
  Looked like a log!

"I had to cross that bog, yer see,
And bluey I was humpin';
But wonderin' what that thing could be
A-layin' there in front o' me
I didn't feel like jumpin'.
Yet, though I shivered like a frog,
  It *seemed* a log!

"I takes a leap and lands right on
The back of that there whopper!"
He stopped. We waited. Then Big Mac
Remarked, "Well, then, what happened, Jack?"
"Not much," said Jack, and drained his grog.
  "It *was* a log!"

W. T. GOODGE

My Old Black Billy

I HAVE humped my bluey in all the States
With my old black billy, the best of mates.
For years I have camped, and toiled, and tramped
On roads that are rough and hilly,
With my plain and sensible,
Indispensable,
Old black billy.

Chorus:
My old black billy, my old black billy,
Whether the wind is warm or chilly
I always find when the shadows fall
My old black billy the best mate of all.

I have carried my swag on the parched Paroo
Where water is scarce and the houses few,
On many a track, in the great Out Back
Where the heat would drive you silly
I've carried my sensible,
Indispensable,
Old black billy.

When the days of tramping at last are o'er
And I drop my swag at the Golden Door,
Saint Peter will stare when he sees me there.
Then he'll say "Poor wandering Willie,
Come in with your sensible,
Indispensable,
Old black billy.''

EDWARD HARRINGTON

ALONG THAT WINDING TRACK

Percy Lindsay.

From The Shearing of the Cook's Dog

THE dog was a little conservative mongrel poodle, with long dirty white hair all over him—longest and most over his eyes, which glistened through it like black beads. Also he seemed to have a bad liver. He always looked as if he was suffering from a sense of injury, past or to come. It did come. He used to follow the shearers up to the shed after breakfast every morning, but he couldn't have done this for love—there was none lost between him and the men. He wasn't an affectionate dog; it wasn't his style. He would sit close against the shed wall for an hour or two, and hump himself, and sulk, and look sick, and snarl whenever the "Sheep-Ho" dog passed, or a man took notice of him. Then he'd go home. What he wanted at the shed at all was only known to himself; no one asked him to come. Perhaps he came to collect evidence against us. The cook called him "my darg", and the men called the cook "Curry-and-Rice", with "old" before it mostly.

.　　.　　.　　.　　.　　.　　.　　.

They chyacked the cook occasionally, and grumbled—or pretended to grumble—about their tucker, and then he'd make a roughly pathetic speech, with many references to his age, and the hardness of his work, and the smallness of his wages, and the inconsiderateness of the men. Then the joker of the shed would sympathize with the cook with his tongue and one side of his face—and joke with the other.

One day in the shed, during smoke-ho the devil whispered to a shearer named Geordie that it would be a lark to shear the cook's dog—the Evil One having previously arranged that the dog should be there, sitting close to Geordie's pen, and that the shearer should have a fine lamb comb on his machine. The idea was communicated through Geordie to his mates, and met with entire and general approval; and for five or ten minutes the air was kept alive by shouting and laughter of the men, and the protestations of the dog. When the shearer touched skin, he yelled "Tar!" and when he finished he shouted "Wool away!" at the top of his voice, and his mates echoed him with a will. A picker-up gathered the fleece with a great show of labour and care, and tabled it, to the well-ventilated disgust of old Scotty, the wool-roller. When they let the dog go he struck for home—a clean-shaven poodle, except for a ferocious moustache and a tuft at the end of his tail.

The cook's assistant said that he'd have given a five-pound note for a portrait of Curry-and-Rice when that poodle came back from the shed. The cook was naturally very indignant; he was surprised at first—then he got mad. He had the whole afternoon to get worked up in, and at tea-time he went for the men properly.

"Wotter yer growlin' about?" asked one. "Wot's the matter with yer, anyway?"

"I don't know nothing about yer dog!" protested a rouseabout; "wotyer gettin' on to me for?"

"Wotter they bin doin' to the cook now?" inquired a ringleader innocently, as he sprawled into his place at the table. "Can't yer let Curry alone? Wot d'yer want to be chyackin' him for? Give it a rest."

"Well, look here, chaps," observed Geordie, in a determined tone, "I call it a shame, that's what I call it. Why couldn't you leave an old man's dog alone? It was a mean, dirty trick to do, and I suppose you thought it funny. You ought to be ashamed of yourselves, the whole lot of you, for a drafted mob of crawlers. If I'd been there it wouldn't have been done; and I wouldn't blame Curry if he was to poison the whole convicted push."

General lowering of faces and pulling of hats down over eyes, and great working of knives and forks; also sounds like men trying not to laugh.

"Why couldn't you play a trick on another man's darg?" said Curry. "It's no use tellin' me. I can see it all as plain as if I was on the board—all of you runnin' and shoutin' an' cheerin' an' laughin', and all over shearin' and ill-usin' a poor little darg! Why couldn't you play a trick on another man's darg? . . . It doesn't matter much—I'm nearly done cookin' here now. . . ."

Geordie bowed his head and ate as though he had a cud, like a cow, and could chew at leisure. He seemed ashamed, as indeed we all were—secretly. Poor old Curry's oft-repeated appeal, "Why couldn't you play a trick with another man's dog?" seemed to have something pathetic about it. The men didn't notice that it lacked philanthropy and logic, and probably the cook didn't notice it either, else he wouldn't have harped on it. Geordie lowered his face, and just then, as luck or the devil would have it, he caught sight of the dog. Then he exploded.

The cook usually forgot all about it in an hour, and then, if you asked him what the chaps had been doing, he'd say, "Oh, nothing! nothing! Only their larks!" But this time he didn't; he was narked for three days, and the chaps marvelled much and were sorry, and treated him with great respect and consideration. They hadn't thought he'd take it so hard—the dog-shearing business—else they wouldn't have done it. They were a little puzzled too, and getting a trifle angry, and would shortly be prepared to take the place of the injured party, and make things unpleasant for the cook. However, he brightened up towards the end of the week, and then it all came out.

"I wouldn't 'a' minded so much," he said, standing by the table with a dipper in one hand, a bucket in the other, and a smile on his face. "I wouldn't 'a' minded so much only they'll think me a flash man in Bourke with that theer darg trimmed up like that!"

HENRY LAWSON

The Shearer's Wife

BEFORE the glare o' dawn I rise
  To milk the sleepy cows, an' shake
The droving dust from tired eyes,
  Look round the rabbit traps, then bake
    The children's bread.
  There's hay to stook, an' beans to hoe,
An' ferns to cut i' th' scrub below;
Women must work, when men must go
  Shearing from shed to shed.
I patch an' darn, now evening comes,
An' tired I am with labour sore,
Tired o' the bush, the cows, the gums,
Tired, but must dree for long months more
    What no tongue tells.
The moon is lonely in the sky,
Lonely the bush, an' lonely I
Stare down the track no horse draws nigh
    An' start . . . at the cattle bells.

LOUIS ESSON

Saltbush Bill, J.P.

BEYOND the land where Leichhardt went,
    Beyond Sturt's Western track,
The rolling tide of change has sent
    Some strange J.P.s Out Back.

And Saltbush Bill, grown old and grey,
    And worn for want of sleep,
Received the news in camp one day
    Behind the travelling sheep

That Edward Rex, confiding in
    His known integrity,
By hand and seal on parchment skin
    Had made him a J.P.

He read the news with eager face
    But found no word of pay.
"I'd like to see my sister's place
    And kids on Christmas day.

"I'd like to see green grass again,
    And watch clear water run,
Away from this unholy plain,
    And flies, and dust, and sun."

At last one little clause he found
    That might some hope inspire,
"A magistrate may charge a pound
    For inquest on a fire."

A big blacks' camp was built close by,
    And Saltbush Bill, says he,
"I think that camp might well supply
    A job for a J.P."

That night, by strange coincidence,
   A most disastrous fire
Destroyed the country residence
   Of Jacky Jack, Esquire.

'Twas mostly leaves, and bark, and dirt;
   The party most concerned
Appeared to think it wouldn't hurt
   If forty such were burned.

Quite otherwise thought Saltbush Bill,
   Who watched the leaping flame.
"The home is small," said he, "but still
   The principle's the same.

"Midst palaces though you should roam,
   Or follow pleasure's tracks,
You'll find," he said, "no place like home—
   At least like Jacky Jack's.

"Tell every man in camp 'Come quick,'
   Tell every black Maria
I give tobacco, half a stick—
   Hold inquest long-a fire."

Each juryman received a name
   Well suited to a Court.
"Long Jack" and "Stumpy Bill" became
   "John Long" and "William Short".

While such as "Tarpot", "Bullock Dray",
   And "Tommy Wait-a-While",
Became, for ever and a day,
   "Scott", "Dickens", and "Carlyle".

And twelve good sable men and true
   Were soon engaged upon
The conflagration that o'erthrew
   The home of John A. John.

Their verdict, "Burnt by act of Fate",
  They scarcely had returned
When, just behind the magistrate,
  Another humpy burned!

The jury sat again and drew
  Another stick of plug.
Said Saltbush Bill, "It's up to you
  Put some one long-a Jug."

"I'll camp the sheep," he said, "and sift
  The evidence about."
For quite a week he couldn't shift,
  The way the fires broke out.

The jury thought the whole concern
  As good as any play.
They used to "take him oath" and earn
  Three sticks of plug a day.

At last the tribe lay down to sleep
  Homeless, beneath a tree;
And onward with his travelling sheep
  Went Saltbush Bill, J.P.

The sheep delivered, safe and sound,
  His horse to town he turned,
And drew some five-and-twenty pound
  For fees that he had earned.

And where Monaro's ranges hide
  Their little farms away—
His sister's children by his side—
  He spent his Christmas Day.

The next J.P. that went Out Back
  Was shocked, or pained, or both,
At hearing every pagan black
  Repeat the juror's oath.

No matter though he turned and fled
  They followed faster still;
"You make it inkwich, boss," they said,
  "All same like Saltbush Bill."

They even said they'd let him see
  The fires originate.
When he refused they said that he
  Was "No good magistrate".

And out beyond Sturt's Western track,
  And Leichhardt's farthest tree,
They wait till fate shall send them back
  Their Saltbush Bill, J.P.

A. B. ("Banjo") PATERSON

From **The Merino Sheep**

EOPLE have got the impression that the merino is a gentle, bleating animal that gets its living without trouble to anybody, and comes up every year to be shorn with a pleased smile upon its amiable face. It is my purpose here to exhibit the merino sheep in its true light.

First let us give him his due. No one can accuse him of being a ferocious animal. No one could ever say that a sheep attacked him without provocation; although there is an old bush story of a man who was discovered in the act of killing a neighbour's wether.

"Hello!" said the neighbour, "What's this? Killing my sheep! What have you got to say for yourself?"

"Yes," said the man, with an air of virtuous indignation. "I *am* killing your sheep. I'll kill *any* man's sheep that bites *me*!"

But as a rule the merino refrains from using his teeth on people. He goes to work in another way.

The truth is that he is a dangerous monomaniac, and his one idea is to ruin the man who owns him. With this object in view he will display a talent for getting into trouble and a genius for dying that are almost incredible.

If a mob of sheep see a bush fire closing round them, do they run away out of danger? Not at all: they rush round and round in a ring till the fire burns them up. If they are in a river-bed, with a howling flood coming down, they will stubbornly refuse to cross three inches of water to save themselves. Dogs may bark and men may shriek, but the sheep won't move. They will wait there till the flood comes and drowns them all, and then their corpses go down the river on their backs with their feet in the air.

A mob will crawl along a road slowly enough to exasperate a snail, but let a lamb get away in a bit of rough country, and a racehorse can't head him back again. If sheep are put into a big paddock with water in three corners of it, they will resolutely crowd into the fourth, and die of thirst.

When being counted out at a gate, if a scrap of bark be left on the ground in the gateway, they will refuse to step over it until dogs and men have sweated and toiled and sworn and "heeled 'em up", and "spoke to 'em", and fairly jammed them at it. At last one will gather courage, rush at the fancied obstacle, spring over it about six feet in the air, and dart away. The next does exactly the same, but jumps a bit higher. Then comes a rush of them following one another in wild bounds like antelopes, until one over-jumps himself and alights on his head. This frightens those still in the yard, and they stop running out.

Then the dogging and shrieking and hustling and tearing have to be gone through all over again. (This on a red-hot day, mind you, with clouds of blinding dust about, the yolk of wool irritating your eyes, and, perhaps, three or four thousand sheep to put through). The delay throws out the man who is counting, and he forgets whether he left off at 45 or 95. The dogs, meanwhile, have taken the first chance to slip over the fence and hide in the shade somewhere, and then there are loud whistlings and oaths, and calls for Rover and Bluey. At last a dirt-begrimed man jumps over the fence, unearths Bluey, and hauls him back by the ear. Bluey sets to work barking and heeling-'em up again, and pretends that he thoroughly enjoys it; but all the while he is looking out for another chance to "clear". And *this* time he won't be discovered in a hurry.

There is a well-authenticated story of a shipload of sheep that was lost because an old ram jumped overboard, and all the rest followed him. No doubt they did, and were proud to do it. A sheep won't go through an open gate on his own responsibility, but he would gladly and proudly "follow the leader" through the red-hot portals of Hades: and it makes no difference whether the lead goes voluntarily, or is hauled struggling and kicking and fighting every inch of the way.

For pure, sodden stupidity there is no animal like the merino. A lamb will follow a bullock-dray, drawn by sixteen bullocks and driven by a profane person with a whip, under the impression that the aggregate monstrosity is his mother. A ewe never knows her own lamb by sight, and apparently has no sense of colour. She can recognize its voice half a mile off among a thousand other voices apparently exactly similar; but when she gets within five yards of it she starts to smell all the other lambs within reach, including the black ones—though her own may be white.

The fiendish resemblance which one sheep bears to another is a great advantage to them in their struggles with their owners. It makes it more difficult to draft them out of a strange flock, and much harder to tell when any are missing.

Concerning this resemblance between sheep, there is a story told of a fat old Murrumbidgee squatter who gave a big price for a famous ram called Sir Oliver. He took a friend out one day to inspect Sir Oliver, and overhauled that animal with a most impressive air of sheep-wisdom.

"Look here," he said, "at the fineness of the wool. See the serrations in each thread of it. See the density of it. Look at the way his legs and belly are clothed—he's wool all over, that sheep, Grand animal, grand animal!"

Then they went and had a drink, and the old squatter said, "Now, I'll show you the difference between a champion ram and a second-rater." So he caught a ram and pointed out his defects. "See here—not half the serrations that other sheep had. No density of fleece to speak of. Bare-bellied as a pig, compared with Sir Oliver. Not that this isn't a fair sheep, but he'd be dear at one-tenth Sir Oliver's price. By the way, Johnson" (to his overseer), "what ram *is* this?"

"That, sir," replied the astounded functionary—"that *is* Sir Oliver, sir!"

.   .   .   .

The hard, resentful look on the faces of all bushmen comes from a long course of dealing with merino sheep. The merino dominates the bush, and gives to Australian literature its melancholy tinge, its despairing pathos. The poems about dying boundary-riders, and lonely graves under mournful she-oaks, are the direct outcome of the poet's too close association with that soul-destroying animal. A man who could write anything cheerful after a day in the drafting-yards would be a freak of nature.

A. B. ("Banjo") PATERSON

On Monday We've Mutton

YOU may talk of the dishes of Paris renown,
  Or for plenty through London may range,
  If variety's pleasing, oh, leave either town,
  And come to the bush for a change.

On Monday we've mutton, with damper and tea;
On Tuesday, tea, damper and mutton,
Such dishes I'm certain all men must agree
Are fit for peer, peasant, or glutton.

On Wednesday we've damper, with mutton and tea;
On Thursday tea, mutton and damper,
On Friday we've mutton, tea, damper, while we
With our flocks over hill and dale scamper.

Our Saturday feast may seem rather strange,
'Tis of damper with tea and fine mutton;
Now surely I've shown you that plenty of change
In the bush, is the friendly board put on.

But no, rest assured that another fine treat
Is ready for all men on one day,
For every bushman is sure that he'll meet
With the whole of the dishes on Sunday.

F. LANCELOTT

The Shearing-Shed

"THE ladies are coming," the super says
    To the shearers sweltering there,
And "the ladies" means in the shearing-shed:
    "Don't cut 'em too bad. Don't swear."
The ghost of a pause in the shed's rough heart,
    And lower is bowed each head;
Then nothing is heard save a whispered word
    And the roar of the shearing-shed.

The tall, shy rouser has lost his wits;
    His limbs are all astray;
He leaves a fleece on the shearing-board
    And his broom in the shearer's way.
There's a curse in store for that jackeroo
    As down by the wall he slants—
But the ringer bends with his legs askew
    And wishes he'd "patched them pants".

They are girls from the city. Our hearts rebel
    As we squint at their dainty feet,
While they gush and say in a girly way
    That "the dear little lambs" are "sweet".
And Bill the Ringer, who'd scorn the use
    Of a childish word like damn,
Would give a pound that his tongue were loose
    As he tackles a lively lamb.

Swift thought of home in the coastal towns—
    Or rivers and waving grass—
And a weight on our hearts that we cannot define
    That comes as the ladies pass;
But the rouser ventures a nervous dig
    With his thumb in the next man's back;
And Bogan says to his pen-mate: "Twig
    The style of that last un, Jack."

Jack Moonlight gives her a careless glance—
    Then catches his breath with pain;
His strong hand shakes, and the sunbeams dance
    As he bends to his work again.
But he's well disguised in a bristling beard,
    Bronzed skin, and his shearer's dress;
And whatever he knew or hoped or feared
    Was hard for his mates to guess.

Jack Moonlight, wiping his broad, white brow,
    Explains, with a doleful smile,
"A stitch in the side," and "I'm all right now"—
    But he leans on the beam awhile,
And gazes out in the blazing noon
    On the clearing, brown and bare . . . .
She had come and gone—like a breath of June
    In December's heat and glare.

HENRY LAWSON

HIS GIRL WILL MEET HIM

Ballad of Mabel Clare

YE children of the Land of Gold,
  I sing this song to you,
And if the jokes are somewhat old
  The central facts are new.
So be it sung, by hut and tent,
  Where tall the native grows;
And understand, the song is meant
  For singing through the nose.

There dwelt a hard old cockatoo
  On western hills far out,
Where everything is green and blue
  (Except, of course, in drought);
A crimson Anarchist was he—
  Held other men in scorn—
Yet preached that every man is free,
  And also "ekal born".

He lived in his ancestral hut—
  His missus wasn't there—
There was none other with him but
  His daughter, Mabel Clare.
Her eyes and hair were like the sun;
  Her foot was like a mat;
Her cheeks a trifle overdone;
  She was a democrat.

A manly independence, born
  Among the hills, she had;
She treated womankind with scorn,
  And often cursed her dad.
She hated swells and shining lights,
  For she had seen a few,
And she believed in Women's Rights
  (She mostly got 'em, too).

A stranger on the neighbouring run
    Sojourned, the squatter's guest;
He was unknown to anyone,
    But exquisitely dress'd;
He wore the latest toggery,
    The loudest thing in ties—
'Twas generally reckoned he
    Was something in disguise.

Once strolling in the noontide heat
    Beneath the blinding glare,
This noble stranger chanced to meet
    The radiant Mabel Clare.
She saw at once he was a swell—
    According to her lights—
But, ah! 'tis very sad to tell,
    She met him oft of nights.

And, rambling through the moonlit gorge,
    She chatted all the while
Of Ingersoll, and Henry George,
    And Bradlaugh and Carlyle:
In short, he learned to love the girl,
    And things went on like this,
Until he said he was an Earl,
    And asked her to be his.

"Oh, say no more, Lord Kawlinee,
    Oh, say no more!" she said;
"Oh, say no more, Lord Kawlinee,
    I wish that I was dead:
My head is in an awful whirl,
    The truth I dare not tell—
I am a democratic girl,
    And cannot wed a swell!"

"O Love!" he cried, "but you forget
    That you are most unjust;
'Twas not my fault that I was set
    Within the upper crust.
Heed not the yarns the poets tell—
    O Darling, do not doubt
A simple lord can love as well
    As any rouseabout!

"For you I'll give my fortune up—
    I'd go to work for you!
I'll put the money in the cup
    And drop the title, too.
Oh, fly with me! Oh, fly with me
    Across the mountains blue!
Hoh, fly with me! *Hoh, fly with me!*"—
    That very night she flew.

They took the train and journeyed down;
    Across the range they sped
Until they came to Sydney town,
    Where shortly they were wed.
(And still upon the western wild
    Admiring teamsters tell
How Mabel's father cursed his child
    For clearing with a swell).

"What ails my bird this bridal night?"
    Exclaimed Lord Kawlinee;
"What ails my own this bridal night?
    O Love, confide in me!"
"Oh now," she said, "that I am yaws
    You'll let me weep—I must—
For I've betrayed the people's caws
    And joined the upper crust."

Oh, proudly smiled his lordship then—
　　His chimney-pot he floor'd;
"Look up, my love, and smile again,
　　For I am not a lord!"
His eye-glass from his eye he tore,
　　The dickey from his breast,
And turned and stood his bride before—
　　A rouseabout, confess'd!

"Unknown I've loved you long," he said,
　　"And I have loved you true—
A-shearing in a neighbour's shed
　　I learned to worship you.
I do not care for place or pelf,
　　For now, my love, I'm sure
That you will love me for myself
　　And not because I'm poor.

"To prove your love I spent my cheque
　　To buy this swell rig-out;
So fling your arms about my neck
　　For I'm a rouseabout!"
At first she gave a startled cry,
　　Then, safe from Care's alarms,
She sighed a soul-subduing sigh
　　And sank into his arms.

He pawned the togs, and home he took
　　His bride in all her charms;
The proud old cockatoo received
　　The pair with open arms.
And long they lived, the faithful bride,
　　The lowly rouseabout—
And if she wasn't satisfied
　　She never let it out.

　　　　　　　　HENRY LAWSON

Moggy's Wedding

JEMMY Ball, a lucky digger,
Who on Ballarat had been some while,
Resolved that he would cut a figure
Acos he had just made his pile.
He stuck up to a gal named Moggy—
A big stout lass from t'other side;
And though at times she got quite groggy,
He determined she should be his bride.

To ask his mates all to the wedding,
Round the diggings he did pop;
And then to purchase clothes and bedding
He took Moggy to a shop;
And she, resolved to "show her muscle",
Bought satin, lace, and bombazine,
A Tuscan bonnet and a bustle,
And any quantity of crinoline.

On the bridal morn the sun shone brightly,
The guests began then to arrive;
And Jim sang out to Mog so sprightly,
"Come on, old woman, look alive."
Jim was dressed up like a dandy,
With rings his fingers they were full;
And Mog uncorked a case of brandy,
And took a most tremendous pull.

The guests into the tent kept dropping,
And they then prepared to start,
And Jemmy up the lush kept mopping,
And then went for an old spring-cart.
Up got Moggy, and her bonnet
With orange-blossoms round was lined;
But the seat broke slap ven she sat on it,
And pitched her right whop out behind.

Next came a dray, and Sydney Polly
With Jack Johnson up did pop,
And Tony Cheeks, with Adelaide Dolly,
Who kept a little sly-grog shop.
Bill Grummet said then, "Let's be going,"
A black belltopper he did vear;
And when some coves began their joeing,
Crikey! oh, how he did svear.

If you had seen them all alighting,
You would have laughed, upon my life;
But it regularly licked dog-fighting,
When asked if she would be his wife:
This produced a vacant stare from Moggy—
To ask this question is the rule;
"Of course I will," says she, half groggy,
"I comed on purpose, you old fool."

They all then went home rather merry,
Resolved that they'd get drunk that day,
And lots of brandy, port, and sherry,
They managed soon to stow away.
Mog to do her share was able,
And she soon got precious tight;
And stretched blind drunk beneath the table
Was how she spent her wedding night.

CHARLES R. THATCHER

From **Pass Round the Hat**

"BOB," I said, "you're a single man. Why don't you get married and settle down?"

"Well," he said, "I ain't got no wife an' kids, that's a fact. But it ain't my fault."

He may have been right about the wife. But I thought of the look that Alice had given him and—

"Girls seem to like me right enough," he said, "but it don't go no further than that. The trouble is that I'm so long, and I always seem to get shook after little girls. At least there was one little girl in Bendigo that I was properly gone on."

"And wouldn't she have you?"

"Well, it seems not."

"Did you ask her?"

"Oh, yes, I asked her right enough."

"Well, and what did she say?"

"She said it would be redicilus for her to be seen trottin' alongside of a chimbly like me."

"Perhaps she didn't mean that. There are any amount of little women who like tall men."

"I thought of that too—afterwards. P'r'aps she didn't mean it that way. I s'pose the fact of the matter was that she didn't cotton on to me, and wanted to let me down easy. She didn't want to hurt me feelin's, if yer understand—she was a very good-hearted little girl. There's some terrible tall fellers where I come from, and I know two as married little girls."

He seemed a hopeless case.

"Sometimes," he said, "sometimes I wish that I wasn't so blessed long."

HENRY LAWSON

After Johnson's Dance

AFTER Johnson's dance—
　　Don't you recollect?
I says, "Goin' 'ome?"
　　You says, "I expect!"
I says, "So am I!"
　　You says, "Not with me!"
I says, "An' for w'y?"
　Blowed if I could see!
　　You says, "Go to France!"
　　After Johnson's dance.

After Johnson's dance—
　　I says, "Em, you *might!*"
"*Might* I though?" says you,
　　"G'arn, you silly fright!"
Then I kissed you, fair—
　　(How you *did* object!)
Tousled all your hair;
　　Don't you recollect?
　　　Took my bloomin' chance
　　　After Johnson's dance!

After Johnson's dance—
　　Smacked my face, you did!
Then I caught you—so!—
　　Like you was a kid.
"Just do that again—
　　Just you *do*," you says.
You says, "Do it!" plain:
　　An', of course, I *does!*
　　　Who made *that* advance—
　　　After Johnson's dance?

CHARLES H. SOUTER

Mary Called Him "Mister"

THEY'D parted but a year before—she never thought he'd come,
She stammer'd, blushed, held out her hand, and called him "*Mister* Gum".
How could he know that all the while she longed to murmur "John".
He called her "Miss le Brook", and asked how she was getting on.

They'd parted but a year before; they'd loved each other well,
But he'd been to the city, and he came back *such* a swell.
They longed to meet in fond embrace, they hungered for a kiss—
But Mary called him "Mister", and the idiot called her "Miss".

He stood and leaned against the door—a stupid chap was he—
And, when she asked if he'd come in and have a cup of tea,
He looked to left, he looked to right, and then he glanced behind,
And slowly doffed his cabbage-tree, and said he "didn't mind".

She made a shy apology because the meat was tough,
And then she asked if he was sure his tea was sweet enough;
He stirred the tea and sipped it twice, and answered "plenty, quite";
And cut the smallest piece of beef and said that it was "right".

She glanced at him at times and coughed an awkward little cough;
He stared at anything but her and said, "I must be off."
That evening he went riding north—a sad and lonely ride.
She locked herself inside her room, and there sat down and cried.

They'd parted but a year before, they loved each other well—
But she was such a country girl and he was such a swell;
They longed to meet in fond embrace, they hungered for a kiss—
But Mary called him "Mister" and the idiot called her "Miss".

HENRY LAWSON

The Free-Selector's Daughter

I MET her on the Lachlan-side—
　A darling girl I thought her,
And ere I left I swore I'd win
　The free-selector's daughter.

I milked her father's cows a month,
　I brought the wood and water,
I mended all the broken fence,
　Before I won the daughter.

I listened to her father's yarns,
　I did just what I "oughter",
And what *you'll* have to do to win
　A free-selector's daughter.

I broke my pipe and burnt my twist,
　And washed my mouth with water;
I had a shave before I kissed
　The free-selector's daughter.

Then, rising in the frosty morn,
　I brought the cows for Mary,
And when I'd milked a bucketful
　I took it to the dairy.

I poured the milk into the dish
　While Mary held the strainer,
I summoned heart to speak my wish,
　And oh! her blush grew plainer.

I told her I must leave the place,
　I said that I would miss her;
At first she turned away her face,
　And then she let me kiss her.

I put the bucket on the ground,
  And in my arms I caught her:
I'd give the world to hold again
  That free-selector's daughter!

HENRY LAWSON

AND CLEARLY ROSE
ANOTHER DAY

Said Hanrahan

"WE'LL all be rooned," said Hanrahan
In accents most forlorn
Outside the church ere Mass began
One frosty Sunday morn.

The congregation stood about,
Coat-collars to the ears,
And talked of stock and crops and drought
As it had done for years.

"It's lookin' crook," said Daniel Croke;
"Bedad, it's cruke, me lad,
For never since the banks went broke
Has seasons been so bad."

"It's dry, all right," said young O'Neil,
With which astute remark
He squatted down upon his heel
And chewed a piece of bark.

And so around the chorus ran
"It's keepin' dry, no doubt."
"We'll all be rooned," said Hanrahan,
"Before the year is out.

"The crops are done; ye'll have your work
To save one bag of grain;
From here way out to Back-o'-Bourke
They're singin' out for rain.

"They're singin' out for rain," he said,
"And all the tanks are dry."
The congregation scratched its head,
And gazed around the sky.

"There won't be grass, in any case,
Enough to feed an ass;
There's not a blade on Casey's place
As I came down to Mass."

"If rain don't come this month," said Dan,
And cleared his throat to speak—
"We'll all be rooned," said Hanrahan,
"If rain don't come this week."

A heavy silence seemed to steal
On all at this remark;
And each man squatted on his heel,
And chewed a piece of bark.

"We want an inch of rain, we do,"
O'Neil observed at last;
But Croke "maintained" we wanted two
To put the danger past.

"If we don't get three inches, man,
Or four to break this drought,
We'll all be rooned," said Hanrahan,
"Before the year is out."

In God's good time down came the rain;
And all the afternoon
On iron roof and window-pane
It drummed a homely tune.

And through the night it pattered still,
And lightsome, gladsome elves
On dripping spout and window-sill
Kept talking to themselves.

It pelted, pelted all day long,
A-singing at its work,
Till every heart took up the song
Way out to Back-o'-Bourke.

And every creek a banker ran,
And dams filled overtop;
"We'll all be rooned," said Hanrahan,
"If this rain doesn't stop."

And stop it did, in God's good time:
And spring came in to fold
A mantle o'er the hills sublime
Of green and pink and gold.

And days went by on dancing feet,
With harvest-hopes immense,
And laughing eyes beheld the wheat
Nid-nodding o'er the fence.

And, oh, the smiles on every face,
As happy lad and lass
Through grass knee-deep on Casey's place
Went riding down to Mass.

While round the church in clothes genteel
Discoursed the men of mark,
And each man squatted on his heel,
And chewed his piece of bark.

"There'll be bush-fires for sure, me man,
There will, without a doubt;
We'll all be rooned," said Hanrahan,
"Before the year is out."

P. J. HARTIGAN
("John O'Brien")

From **Bush Life**

LIFE, after all, is mostly made up of little things, prosaic and unpicturesque. The squatter, for instance, is supposed (in literature) to ride about over his vast domains on a thoroughbred horse, always at full gallop. In the moving pictures, he is generally shown wearing a red shirt and top boots, as those things lend verisimilitude to an otherwise dull and uninteresting narrative. In real life, he rarely rides in anything but a motor car; and if he appeared in a red shirt and top boots, all the emus on the run would follow him for miles, dancing and cavorting about, wondering what strange animal had got in amongst them.

This article then is concerned with the little things of life in the bush, the every-day occurrences which mean so much to the bush people. If we can find therein some humour and some human nature, so much the better. The first picture to be thrown on our screen was roughly sketched in a notebook on a trip to Brewarrina.

West of Dubbo, the West begins. . . . A land of vast distances. Behind us the railway line stretches, straight as an arrow across the plains till the rails seem to run together and disappear in the distance. Ahead of us, it runs on, straight as ever, through a shimmer of haze, till it is lost in a lagoon which is not really a lagoon but a mirage. When these Western people wish to describe the essence of meanness, they say that a man is too mean to give your dog a drink at his mirage.

And who shall describe the eerie loneliness of this country? A few sheep, a few galahs, and a few magpies; these are the only living things, other than human, seen in two hundred miles. Travelling through a station of a hundred thousand sheep, one hardly sees any of them. At little dusty wayside stations the people get in and out—long-legged, thin men, sunburnt to a mahogany colour. Women almost as sunburnt, with quick and earnest faces. The lounge lizard and the baby doll have no place in this life. Two women meet on the platform, get into the carriage, and start a conversation. Of what will they speak? Will they talk about trips to Sydney, about fashions, or about their families? Not a bit of it. One says to the other, "Have you had the mice yet?" And there we get the keynote of bush life. Nature, resenting human invasion, keeps up a sort of guerilla warfare, using such weapons as plagues of mice, grasshoppers, caterpillars, and in

some places even kangaroos and emus. The bushman
and his wife can never go to sleep on the job.

"Have we had the mice?" says her friend. "My dear,
the place is just a mass of mice. We have to hang
everything up by wire hooks to the trees away from the
mice. I pulled back the bed-clothes to put the baby to
sleep and there was a nest of mice in the bed."

"How are the flies with you this season?"

"Pretty bad. We have had to crutch everything and
the boys get so tired after working in the yards all the
week that they won't play tennis on Sundays. We get
tired too. We've been making jam all the week. We
have millions of grapes and figs, but the bees and the
hornets have come down in droves to suck the juice out
of the fruit and we're terrified of getting stung. If you
like to send over, we can give you a couple of clothes-
baskets full of grapes and figs and we would never miss
them."

This is Nature in the West, giving with one hand,
and taking with the other.

The train rattles on. The sun sinks lower in the west,
shedding a coloured light on the dark silver of the
myall-trees and the homely grey of the old-man
saltbush. In this light the krui-bush and the emu-bush
become things of beauty, for they seem to reflect the
rays of the sun. Through the carriage windows the
breeze brings in a scent of pine. Is there anything more
beautiful than the plains in a good season?

The train stops at a little township, and two pass-
engers get in, one obviously a city man and the other a
shy, silent, country youth with hands calloused by
lifting sheep whose fleeces are full of thistles and burr.
Country and City are face to face.

The city man asks him, "Do you happen to know
anything about a place called Gongolgon?" (Pr. Gon-
Gol-Gon)

The answer comes in the true backblock drawl,

"Yairs! I know Gongolgon all right. I come from
near Gongolgon."

"Good. Then perhaps you can give me some information. My company has lent some money on an hotel there—the Woolpack Hotel—but the man has left it, and I want to know how it is getting on. It's the best hotel in Gongolgon, isn't it?"

"Oh yairs! It's the best hotel in Gongolgon all right. There is only one hotel in Gongolgon."

"But I mean it's in a good position—in the main street and all that?"

"Oh yairs! There is only one street in Gongolgon."

"Well, have you seen it lately? Do you know how the place is looking?"

"Well, I wouldn't say it is *too* good."

"Not too good. What do you mean by not too good?"

"Oh, the swagmen has been campin' there and they burned all the floors and the fences an' the counters, an' all that, for firewood. And some chap come along and carted away a lot of the bricks at night. I s'pose he was building somethin'."

"Carted away the bricks! Then is everything gone?"

"Oh no, everything isn't gone. The *foundations* is there all right. They'd come in handy if you wanted to build another pub."

That ended the dialogue. Who shall say that the bush holds no surprises, no breaks in its monotony?

.   .   .   .

A couple of hundred years hence, perhaps, someone will write the history of these early days, a lot of it incredible, or, at the least, difficult of understanding. But when that date arrives, time will have mellowed the past. The man who carted away the Gongolgon hotel, brick by brick, will be as romantic as a Highland raider ... and there will be a terrific demand for samples of old colonial curios—beds with strips of greenhide in the place of springs, and crudely-carved stockwhip handles made of the scented myall wood. Then, and then only, will the bush people come into their own.

A. B. ("Banjo") PATERSON